Maddie
Good Show 6th July 2014
Love Nana + Grampy

my first book of
questions and answers

spacecraft

James Pickering

This is a Parragon Book
First published in 2002

Parragon
Queen Street House
4 Queen Street
Bath BA1 1HE, UK

Produced by

David West ⚥ Children's Books
7 Princeton Court
55 Felsham Road
Putney
London SW15 1AZ

British Library Cataloguing-in-Publication Data

A catalogue record for this book is available from
the British Library.

ISBN 0-75258-458-8

Printed in China

Designers
Axis Design, Aarti Parmar, Rob Shone,
Fiona Thorne

Illustrators
Colin Howard, Terry Riley (SGA)

Cartoonist
Peter Wilks (SGA)

Editor
Ross McLaughness

CONTENTS

Who invented the first rockets?

Small firework-like rockets were invented in China about 1,000 years ago. The Chinese used to fire them at their enemies during battles.

Which rocket first used liquid fuel?

Robert Goddard launched the first liquid-fuelled rocket in 1926. His rocket only went 12.5 m into the air (about as high as seven tall people), and landed 64 m away. All spacecraft are launched using liquid fuel rockets.

Robert Goddard

? Why do spacecraft need rockets?

Jet engines and petrol engines need air to work. They would be no use in space, because there's no air in space. Rocket engines don't need air, so they can work just as well in space as they do on Earth.

Ariane rocket

?What is a satellite?

A satellite is any object which orbits (travels round and round) the Earth. The Earth's natural satellite is the Moon. The first man-made satellite was Sputnik 1, which was launched in 1957.

Sputnik 1

?How do satellites use the Sun?

Satellites can carry on working for a long time because the Sun gives them energy. Satellites have solar panels, like wings, which soak up light and heat from the Sun, and turn them into electricity.

Solar panels

? What do satellites do?

Satellites do lots of jobs. Some of them take pictures of Earth to tell us about the weather, and some are used for spying on other countries.

Communications satellites bounce television and telephone signals back to Earth.

Telstar communications satellite

TRUE OR FALSE?

Outer space is very windy.

FALSE. There is no air or wind in space. The flag on the Moon had to be held up with a wire, so that it looked as if it was blowing in the wind.

Outer space is freezing cold.

TRUE. Outer space is very cold indeed, unless the Sun's shining on you, when it's extremely hot.

Who was the first astronaut?

The first earthling in space wasn't a person – it was a Russian dog called Laika. She spent seven days orbiting the Earth aboard a small spacecraft called Sputnik 2 in 1957. Laika's journey proved that space flight would be safe for humans.

Laika

Who was the first person in space?

Russian pilot Yuri Gagarin became the first person in space in 1961. He orbited the Earth once in a Vostok 1 spacecraft. His journey only took an hour and a half. He was given a hero's welcome when he returned to Earth.

Yuri Gagarin

? Who went back to space after 36 years?

John Glenn became the first American to orbit the Earth in 1962, when he was 41 years old. 36 years later, he went back, and became the oldest ever astronaut. He carried out experiments to see if space travel was more dangerous for older people.

John Glenn

Laika was the only animal in space.

FALSE. Spiders, bees, shrimps, chimpanzees, tortoises, frogs, goldfish and jellyfish have all been to space.

You can walk in space.

TRUE. The first space-walk was by a Russian astronaut in 1965. He was roped to his spacecraft.

Why do astronauts need space suits?

Space suits protect astronauts from the extreme heat and cold of space, and from dangerous radiation. They also give astronauts air to breathe, and stop their bodies from exploding!

How do astronauts repair satellites?

Astronauts repair satellites using the smallest of all manned spacecraft – the Manned Manoeuvring Unit (MMU). The astronaut straps on the MMU, and flies through space, using 24 small jets of gas.

MMU in action

Astronauts' helmets are made of gold.

TRUE. At least the visors are. A gold tint protects astronauts' eyes from very strong sunlight.

There's rubbish in space.

TRUE. There are thousands of disused satellites and other dangerous pieces of junk whizzing around the Earth.

? Why do things float around in space?

You don't float around here on Earth, because gravity is always pulling you towards the Earth's surface. In outer space, far away from other worlds, there's no gravity, so everything floats around, including astronauts!

Saturn 5
rocket

? Why are rockets so huge?

Rockets have to travel very quickly to escape the Earth's atmosphere and reach space. They need huge rocket engines and thousands of tonnes of fuel to reach high speed. Saturn 5 rockets were as high as a 25 storey skyscraper!

? Are rockets re-usable?

Most rockets aren't re-usable. When they've run out of fuel, they drop away, never to be used again. But the space shuttle uses two re-usable rocket boosters, which parachute back to Earth.

Shuttle launch

Rockets only travel in space.

FALSE. The Blue Flame was a record-breaking rocket car, which could travel at over 1,000 kph – as fast as a jet plane!

Stages crash back to Earth.

FALSE. Rocket stages get very hot as they return to Earth. They burn up, until there's nothing left.

? *Are rockets all in one piece?*

Rockets are made up of several pieces, or stages. The lower stages contain fuel and rocket engines. When they run out of fuel, they're no longer needed. So each empty stage drops away, one by one.

Who first landed on the Moon?

American astronaut Neil Armstrong was the first person to set foot on the Moon in 1969. He landed his Eagle spacecraft, and, along with Buzz Aldrin, spent about two and a half hours exploring the rocky surface, before flying back home.

Moon rock

What did astronauts find on the Moon?

Astronauts collected Moon rocks and soil, and brought them back to Earth to be studied. Two astronauts even found an unmanned probe, which had been sent to the Moon two years earlier.

? Who drove a car on the Moon?

A team of astronauts in 1971 drove around on the Moon in a Lunar Rover car. They were able to explore much further than on foot, and collect plenty of rocks.

Lunar Rover

Apollo 13

❓ What can you see from the Moon?

The sky over the Moon is always black. The Earth seems very large and bright, as it rises and sets over the horizon. You can also see the Sun and the stars.

❓ Who didn't make it to the Moon?

There was an explosion aboard the Apollo 13 spacecraft, during a trip to the Moon. The crew were ordered to return to Earth. They only just made it home before they ran out of air.

The Moon is covered in water.

FALSE. The Moon has several 'seas' but they're full of rocks and dust, not water. But scientists think there might be frozen water at the Moon's poles.

Russian astronauts have visited the Moon.

FALSE. Twelve astronauts have walked on the Moon – all of them were American.

? How long did it take to reach the Moon?

Our nearest neighbour, the Moon, is about 384,000 km from the Earth. Even with the help of fast and powerful rockets, astronauts had to sit in their spacecraft for four and a half days before they reached the Moon.

Astronauts on the Mir space station

? How do you eat in space?

Astronauts take dried food into space. They add water, to turn it into a proper meal. You have to eat carefully in space, in case your food floats off the plate!

? Can people live in space?

People have stayed in space stations for over a year, but space travel can be bad for your health. Astronauts' bones, hearts and muscles become weak unless they take plenty of exercise.

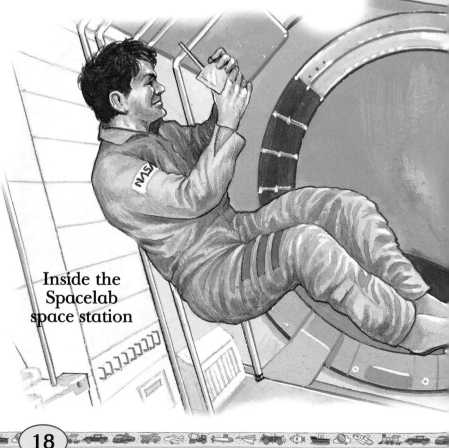

Inside the Spacelab space station

❓ What happens when space stations close down?

Once space stations are abandoned, they usually fall back to Earth, and burn up in the atmosphere. But the American Skylab space station didn't burn up, and parts of it fell on to farmland in Australia.

Skylab burning up

Which spacecraft can be used again?

Early spacecraft could only be used once, but the American space shuttle and the Russian Buran spaceplane were designed to be used many times. Six space shuttles have been built. Between them, they have made over 100 space flights.

Space shuttle

What is the shuttle used for?

Early shuttle missions carried large satellites into space. But after the shuttle Challenger exploded in 1986, scientists thought it would be safer to use unmanned rockets to launch satellites. These days, the shuttle is used for satellite repair, building a space station and finding out more about space.

❓ What is a robot arm?

❓ The shuttle has a 15 m-long arm, which is used to grab satellites and other objects in space, and put them into the shuttle. Just like your arms, it has shoulder, elbow and wrist joints. Astronauts can even hitch a ride on the arm!

Robot arm

Who landed in the sea?

Astronauts on all the early American space missions parachuted into the sea in their capsules. Navy ships or helicopters kept in touch with the astronauts, collected them, and took them safely back to shore.

What is mission control?

Mission control is the name for the team of scientists and space experts on Earth, who control every space mission. Mission control talks to astronauts by radio, giving them orders and helping out in emergencies.

Mission control

❓ *How do spacecraft return to Earth?*

Spacecraft get very hot when they enter the Earth's atmosphere. The shuttle is covered in heat-proof tiles to protect it. It lands on a runway, just like a normal aeroplane.

Shuttle returning to Earth

What used balloons to land on Mars?

The Pathfinder probe parachuted on to Mars inside some balloons. When the balloons deflated, a robot car called Sojourner drove away over them.

Pathfinder probe

What is a space probe?

Voyager probe

A space probe is an unmanned spacecraft, which sends pictures of other planets and their moons back to Earth. Some probes, such as Pathfinder, land on other planets. The Voyager probes flew past the planets, and are now heading towards the stars.

Giotto probe

? Which probe chased a comet?

The Giotto probe chased
Halley's comet when it passed
Earth in 1986. Giotto proved
that the comet was a large,
dirty snowball, orbiting the
Sun. To protect it from the
comet's long, dusty tail,
Giotto had a special shield.

Is there a space telescope?

The Hubble space telescope was launched by a space shuttle in 1990. On Earth, the view of the stars is often spoilt by pollution and street lights. In space, Hubble doesn't have these problems, so it sends us amazing pictures.

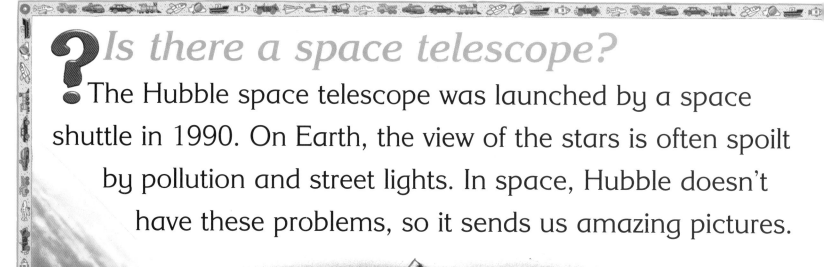

Hubble space
telescope

Eagle Nebula

❓ *What can Hubble see?*

The Hubble space telescope can see a very long way into space. It has taken pictures of the Eagle Nebula – a massive cloud of gas. Inside the fingers of cloud, the gas is gathering together to make new stars. Hubble is so sensitive, it could spot a coin 640 km away!

Hubble needed to wear glasses.

TRUE. Hubble couldn't see very well at first. Astronauts gave it new lenses, which work like glasses, and it can see much better now.

Hubble has seen alien spacecraft.

FALSE. Hubble has taken pictures of stars in distant parts of the Universe, but it hasn't found any sign of alien life.

? What will spacecraft look like in the future?

The space shuttle is very expensive to launch. American scientists think that the VentureStar space plane might be cheaper. VentureStar could be used to launch other spacecraft in orbit.

VentureStar

Underwater training

? How can I become an astronaut?

You have to train for several years to become an astronaut. Here on Earth, astronauts practice space-walking in water tanks. This gives them an idea of how floating in space will feel.

? Will there be cities in space?

One day, spacecraft might be used to build cities or even hotels in space. Once the International Space Station has been built, it will be a permanent home for astronauts.

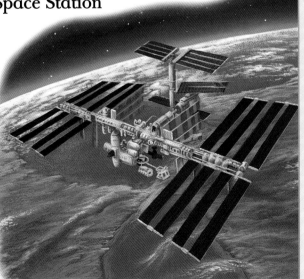

International Space Station

Huygens probe

? Is there life on other planets?

Scientists are sure there isn't life on any planet near Earth. But there might be on one of Saturn's moons – Titan. The Huygens probe will parachute on to Titan in 2004 to look for any signs of life.

? Will people ever live on other planets?

It might be possible for robots to build airtight buildings on Mars. People could live inside, and grow plants, which would make air and water. Gradually people would be able to live anywhere on the planet.

Mars base of the future

? *Will we ever travel to other stars?*

If a space rocket was sent to the nearest star to our Sun, the journey would last over 150,000 years. We will probably never travel to other stars.

Spacecraft of the future

Index